KINDERGARTEN READING

YAY IT'S TIME TO READ!

Improve Your Child's Reading and Writing Skills With This Kindergarten Workbook

Ages 5-6

SHARON MCLEAN

Copyright © 2021 Sharon Mclean

All Rights Reserved

Copyright 2021 By Sharon Mclean - All rights reserved.

The following book is produced below with the goal of providing information that is as accurate and reliable as possible. Regardless, purchasing this eBook can be seen as consent to the fact that both the publisher and the author of this book are in no way experts on the topics discussed within and that any recommendations or suggestions that are made herein are for entertainment purposes only. Professionals should be consulted as needed prior to undertaking any of the action endorsed herein.

This declaration is deemed fair and valid by both the American Bar Association and the Committee of Publishers Association and is legally binding throughout the United States.

Furthermore, the transmission, duplication or reproduction of any of the following work including specific information will be considered an illegal act irrespective of if it is done electronically or in print. This extends to creating a secondary or tertiary copy of the work or a recorded copy and is only allowed with express written consent from the Publisher. All additional right reserved.

The information in the following pages is broadly considered to be a truthful and accurate account of facts and as such any inattention, use or misuse of the information in question by the reader will render any resulting actions solely under their purview. There are no scenarios in which the publisher or the original author of this work can be in any fashion deemed liable for any hardship or damages that may befall them after undertaking information described herein.

Additionally, the information in the following pages is intended only for informational purposes and should thus be thought of as universal. As befitting its nature, it is presented without assurance regarding its prolonged validity or interim quality. Trademarks that are mentioned are done without written consent and can in no way be considered an endorsement from the trademark holder.

Table of Contents

PART I 4

Chapter 1: Recognize The Sounds 5

   Activity One: Sounding The Alphabet 5

   Activity Two: Their Spoken Sounds 6

   Activity Three: What Is That Sound? 7

   Activity Four: Print The Letter That Matches The Beginning Sound 9

   Activity Five: Trace The Following Letters 10

   Activity Six: What Letter Is Missing? 12

Chapter 2: Consonants 14

   Activity One: Find The Consonants 14

   Activity Two: Fill In The Missing Letter 16

   Activity Three: Circle The Word 17

   Activity Four: Write That Word! 19

   Activity Five: Find The Missing Word! 21

   Activity Six: Write The Word! 22

Chapter 3: Vowels 23

   Activity One: Find The Vowels 23

   Activity Two: Fill In The Missing Letter 25

   Activity Three: Circle That Word! 27

   Activity Four: Write That Word! 28

   Activity Five: Find The Missing Word! 30

   Activity Six: Spell The Word! 32

   Activity Seven: Draw A Picture! 33

Chapter 4: Phonemes 35

   Activity One: What Is The Difference? 35

   Activity Two: Sound And Write 37

   Activity Three: Sound Out These Words 39

   Activity Four: Fill In The Missing Word 40

   Activity Five: Draw A Picture 42

   Activity Six: Spot The Missing Letter 42

   Activity One: Do They Rhyme? 44

   Activity Two: Match The Rhyming Words 46

   Activity Three: Find A Rhyming Word 48

   Activity Four: Write The Rhyme 49

   Activity Five: Do They Rhyme? 51

   Activity Six: Draw A Picture! 53

Chapter 1: Ricky Responsibility 56

Chapter 2: Hannah Learns About Hard Work 58

Chapter 3: Chester Gains His Confidence! 61

Chapter 4: Carly Learns to Communicate 64

Chapter 5: Lester Learns a Lesson About Love 66

Chapter 6: Felicia Spends Time With Family 68

Chapter 7: Sean Gets Sick 70

Chapter 8: Melissa Makes a New Friend 73

Chapter 9: Austin Learns to Care for Animals 77

Chapter 10: Chelsea Discovers Consistency 81

Chapter 11: Barney Becomes Brave 83

Chapter 12: Talia Learns About Team Work..84

Poems 178

PART I

Chapter 1: Recognize The Sounds

Recognizing the sounds is an important first step to reading! By recognizing the sounds of each letter, you can learn to read phonetically. This means you can sound each letter out until you discover the words you are reading!

Activity One: Sounding The Alphabet

Below you will find all 26 letters and the sounds of each letter. See if you can sound them out!

A ("aye")   B ("bee")   C ("c")   D ("dee")

E ("ee")   F ("eff")   G ("gee")   H ("aych")

I ("eye")   J ("jay")   K ("kay")   L ("ell")

M ("em")   N ("en")   O ("oh")   P ("pee")

Q ("cue")   R ("are")   S ("ess")   T ("tee")

U ("you")   V ("vee")   W ("double you")

X ("ex")   Y ("why")   Z ("zee")

Activity Two: Their Spoken Sounds

Now that you know how to sound out the alphabet, its time to sound out the alphabet using phonetics. This means you will sound out the alphabet based on how they sound inside of words!

A	B	C	D	E	F	G
H	I	J	K	L	M	N
O	P	Q	R	S	T	U
V	W	X	Y	Z		

Activity Three: What Is That Sound?

Have a grown up read the following words. See if you can identify what letter the word starts with, based on how it sounds.

- Pig

- Rainbow
- Fish
- Hotdog
- Baseball Bat
- Clown
- Frog
- Bird
- Spider Web
- Glasses
- Owl
- Hamster
- Bumble Bee
- Snake
- Lion
- Crab
- Apple
- Burger
- Sandwich
- Banana
- Castle
- Egg
- Ice Cream
- Mushroom
- Fork
- Key
- Pear

Activity Four: Print The Letter That Matches The Beginning Sound

Have a grown up read the following words out to you. Then, print out the letter that matches the beginning sound of the word.

- Sun
- Baseball Bat
- Orange
- Mushroom
- Penguin
- Flag
- Elephant
- Pizza
- Cat
- Heart
- Rainbow
- Kite
- Leaf
- Guitar
- Balloon
- Present
- Toque
- Snake
- Spider Web
- Mushroom
- Owl

- Lion
- Frog
- Igloo
- Duck
- Ice Cream
- Traffic Light
- Umbrella
- Whale
- Peach

Activity Five: Trace The Following Letters

Trace the following groups of letters.

Group 1) A A A A A a a a a a

Group 2) B B B B B b b b b b

Group 3) C C C C C c c c c c

Group 4) D D D D D d d d d d

Group 5) E E E E E e e e e e

Group 6) F F F F F f f f f f

Group 7) G G G G G g g g g g

Group 8) H H H H H h h h h h

Group 9) I I I I I i i i i i

Group 10) J J J J J j j j j

Group 11) K K K K K k k k k

Group 12) L L L L L l l l l

Group 13) M M M M M m m m m

Group 14) N N N N N n n n n

Group 15) O O O O O o o o o

Group 16) P P P P P p p p p

Group 17) Q Q Q Q Q q q q q

Group 18) R R R R R r r r r

Group 19) S S S S S s s s s

Group 20) T T T T T t t t t

Group 21) U U U U U u u u u

Group 22) V V V V V v v v v

Group 23) W W W W W w w w w

Group 24) X X X X X x x x x

Group 25) Y Y Y Y Y y y y y

Group 26) Z Z Z Z Z z z z z

Activity Six: What Letter Is Missing?

Find the missing letter in the following groups of words!

Group 1) Cake, b_ke, l_ke, s_ke.

Group 2) L_g, d_g, bog, h_g.

Group 3) C_t, hat, b_t, s_t, f_t.

Group 4) Tap, l_p, m_p, c_p.

Group 5) R_g, mug, d_g, h_g, b_g.

Group 6) Had, b_d, s_d, d_d.

Group 7) H_n, p_n, ten, d_n.

Group 8) Pig, j_g, b_g, r_g.

Group 9) M_t, cat, h_t, b_t.

Group 10) H_t, s_t, p_t, fit.

Group 11) Log, b_g, d_g, h_g.

Group 12) Hip, l_p, s_p, d_p.

Group 13) W_t, g_t, bet, s_t.

Group 14) M_g, b_g, d_g, hug.

Group 15) Had, b_d, d_d, m_d.

Group 16) Pen, h_n, d_n, t_n.

Group 17) T_n, ran, c_n, p_n.

Group 18) Dot, r_t, h_t, n_t.

Group 19) S_ke, c_ke, rake, l_ke.

Group 20) Fog, j_g, l_g, b_g.

Group 21) M_t, cat, h_t, r_t.

Group 22) Wet, g_t, l_t, m_t.

Group 23) R_g, mug, h_g, d_g.

Group 24) D_g, hog, f_g, l_g.

Group 25) Hip, l_p, s_p, sh_p.

Group 26) H_d, b_d, rad, d_d.

Group 27) Fox, b_x, l_x, _x.

Group 28) Mow, s_w, c_w, h_w.

Group 29) Mug, l_g, j_g, r_g.

Group 30) Dot, h_t, p_t, r_t.

Chapter 2: Consonants

Consonants account for every single letter in the alphabet except for five or six letters of the alphabet. The letters of the alphabet that count as consonants include B, C, D, F, G, H, J, K, L, M, N, P, Q, R, S, T, V, W, X, Y, and Z. Sometimes, Y is considered a vowel, though. Consonants make up the majority of the letters in a word. However, every word must have both consonants and vowels in order to be a true word.

Activity One: Find The Consonants

In the following groups you will see several letters in a row. Circle the ones that are consonants, and leave the ones that are vowels.

Group 1) A, B, C, D, E, F

Group 2) G, H, I, J, K, L

Group 3) M, N, O, P, Q, R, S

Group 4) T, U, V, W, X, Y, Z

Group 5) A, C, E, G, I, K

Group 6) B, D, F, H, J, M

Group 7) N, P, R, T, V, X

Group 8) Y, Z, A, C, E, H

Group 9) A, L, M, O, N, P

Group 10) T, X, Y, A, Z, B

Group 11) G, J, K, M, N, O

Group 12) A, E, I, P, O, U

Group 13) A, P, L, M, O, I

Group 14) Z, Q, R, U, S, T

Group 15) G, L, H, K, I, M

Group 16) A, E, I, O, U, Y

Group 17) B, X, L, O, Z, H

Group 18) P, U, M, E, T, S

Group 19) L, O, I, Z, Q, R

Group 20) T, O, U, Z, S, R

Group 21) I, K, L, M, N, P

Group 22) Q, P, L, R, S, O

Group 23) A, B, C, L, M, O

Group 24) D, L, K, Y, Z, S

Group 25) G, K, J, H, C, E

Group 26) K, S, E, T, I, X

Group 27) X, G, Y, Z , K, E

Group 28) R, S, I, E, O, Z

Group 29) L, K, M, E, N, P

Group 30) B, K, R, S, O, L

Activity Two: Fill In The Missing Letter

Fill in the missing consonant from each of the following words!

1. I am hap_y today.

2. My do_ loves going for walks!

3. Mot_er knows best.

4. I see a cu_cake.

5. The box is _ig.

6. My frie_d loves playing with me.

7. The _umblebee is in the beehive.

8. The lam_ is on.

9. He rides his bi_e really fast!

10. We are ri_ing a raft.

11. I love going cam_ing.

12. Who is hidin_ in the den?

13. My pen is re_.

14. Can you see t_e tree?

15. I love playi_g baseball.

16. That cat is very _at!

17. The ma_ is my dad.

18. A man _as a van.

19. It was a _ery hot pan.

20. My car goe_ very fast!

21. The piz_a had cheese on it.

22. My siste_ loves dolls.

23. Trees have green lea_es.

24. The gar_en is full of flowers.

25. Family din_er is so much fun!

26. Mother sai_ no.

27. The fox lo_es to run.

28. I can jum_ really high!

29. Fis_ love swimming.

30. The sun rises every _orning.

Activity Three: Circle The Word

Circle the words that start with a consonant from each of the following groups!

Group 1) Unicorn, Antelope, Cat

Group 2) Art, Easel, Paintbrush

Group 3) Apple, Banana, Orange

Group 4) Eye, Ear, Leg

Group 5) Elephant, Tiger, Octopus

Group 6) Wood, Earth, Air

Group 7) Farm, Oats, Sky

Group 8) Time, Clock, Watch

Group 9) Baby, Adult, Adolescent

Group 10) Floor, Ceiling, Wall

Group 11) Night, Morning, Early

Group 12) Chicken, Duck, Egg

Group 13) Umbrella, Rain, Wet

Group 14) Table, Plate, Eat

Group 15) Eagle, Hawk, Owl

Group 16) Man, Woman, Child

Group 17) Sandwich, Egg, Toast

Group 18) Anger, Envy, Happiness

Group 19) Beauty, Love, Comfort

Group 20) Antlers, Horns, Moose

Group 21) Alligator, Crocodile, Fish

Group 22) Ankle, Ear, Hand

Group 23) Bakery, Post Office, Hardware Store

Group 24) Uncle, Aunt, Cousin

Group 25) Melon, Cucumber, Eggplant

Group 26) White, Orange, Yellow

Group 27) Water, Oil, Gasoline

Group 28) Ambulance, Helicopter, Hospital

Group 29) Air, Fire, Water

Group 30) Bread, Butter, Jam

Activity Four: Write That Word!

These words start with consonants. Write them yourself!

1. Cat ___

2. Dog ___

3. Bat ___

4. Rag ___

5. Gap ___

6. Jet ___

7. Hog ___

8. Fog ___

9. Bog ___

10. Fox ___

11. Rat ___

12. Map ___

13. Fat ___

14. Ham ___

15. Web ___

16. Den ___

17. Dot ___

18. Mud ___

19. Cub ___

20. Pup ___

21. Mop ___

22. Dad ___

23. Mom ___

24. Gas ___

25. Sap ___

26. Lap ___

27. Pad ___

28. Bin ___

29. Tip ___

30. Wig ___

Activity Five: Find The Missing Word!

Find the missing word in each of the following sentences. Hint: it starts with a consonant!

1. The ___ sleeps upside down. (Bat, ant, elk)

2. I hurt my ___. (Arm, hand, ear.)

3. My shirt is covered in polka ___. (Dots, ants, eyes.)

4. My ___ was once a puppy. (Dog, elephant, owl.)

5. My ___ are so strong! (Eyes, ears, legs.)

6. I can't see outside because of the ___. (Air, orange, fog.)

7. I love drinking ___. (Apples, ants, juice.)

8. ___ is very sticky. (Ear, ask, gum.)

9. ___ are my favorite fruit. (Bananas, apples, oranges.)

10. I love singing ___. (Air, easy, songs.)

11. The ___ rises and sets. (Earth, adult, sun.)

12. I live on top of a ___. (Actor, hill, echo.)

13. The ___ flies south for winter. (Bird, elephant, ant.)

14. He is a ___. (Ambulance, firefighter, elbow.)

15. My ___ are growing! (Feet, eggplant, umbrella.)

16. I eat ___ in the morning. (Easter, breakfast, unicorn.)

17. ___ makes your bones stronger. (Milk, uncle, apple.)

18. The ___ rings. (Ate, you, bell.)

19. Sandwiches are made with ____. (Oat, bread, apple.)

20. I like eating ___. (Cake, uniform, antelope.)

21. Flowers grow in the ____. (Air, garden, eagle.)

22. I go to sleep at ___. (Night, alligator, eggplant.)

23. I color on ___. (Airplane, acorn, paper.)

24. My mother took my ___. (Ear, picture, arm.)

25. ___ live on the farm. (Pigs, egg, asparagus.)

26. I need a ___ of water. (Astronaut, drink, eel.)

27. The ___ blows the leaves away. (Wind, igloo, octopus.)

28. Puddles come from ___. (Ox, rain, apple.)

29. The ____ hops. (Rabbit, orange, elephant.)

30. ___ is very cold. (Ocean, unicorn, snow.)

Activity Six: Write The Word!

Below are words that start with consonants. Write them yourself!

1. Met   2. Tap   3. Lip   4. Mat   5. Bug   6. Bad   7. Ten   8. Set

9. Dot   10. Hip   11. Dog   12. Fog   13. Pig   14. Mad   15. Mat

16. Let   17. Map   18. Sip   19. Rug   20. Had   21. Hen   22. Win

23. Lap   24. Won   25. Jog   26. Mug   27. Wet   28. Pen   29. Cat

30. Say

Chapter 3: Vowels

Vowels are any word that starts with a, e, i, o, u, and sometimes y, when no other vowels are in that word. For example, in the word "By" the y is a vowel, but in the word "Bye" the y is not a vowel because there is an e in that word! Let's see what else you can learn about vowels.

<u>Activity One: Find The Vowels</u>

Find the vowels in the groups of letters below!

Group 1) A B C D F G

Group 2) E H J K L M

Group 3) I N P Q R S

Group 4) T U V W X Y

Group 5) Z B C D E F

Group 6) G H I J K L

Group 7) M N O P Q R

Group 8) S T U V W X

Group 9) Y Z L M N P

Group 10) Q R S T U V

Group 11) A B C X Y Z

Group 12) D E L M N P

Group 13) T U X Y Z W

Group 14) F C H I J K M

Group 15) E R S T X Y

Group 16) Z K L M N O

Group 17) B Q R S T U

Group 18) L Z F R S A

Group 19) I H G N R T

Group 20) O R S F G H

Group 21) I P R S T N

Group 22) S E L O F N

Group 23) D E R K T Y

Group 24) Y S P N D T

Group 25) E R F S H D

Group 26) I M N L P S

Group 27) K H U N D V

Group 28) L S T O R P

Group 29) N U V C B F

Group 30) L K N P E R

Activity Two: Fill In The Missing Letter

Find the missing letter for each of the following words! Hint: the missing letters are all vowels!

1. A stop sign means st_p.

2. The oce_n is full of fish.

3. All_gators live in the water.

4. _gloo's are made of snow and ice.

5. _ranges are a type of fruit, and a color.

6. I love _pple pie.

7. El_phants are ginormous!

8. Dolph_ns live in the ocean.

9. Sandw_ches are great for lunch.

10. When I grow up, I want to be an _stronaut.

11. Squirrels eat _corns.

12. F_sh live in the sea.

13. I wear a sc_rf when it is cold outside.

14. My sister won an aw_rd.

15. C_rrots are an orange vegetable.

16. My d_d drives a red car.

17. My mother we_rs a blue dress.

18. I fly my k_te on windy days.

19. My dog goes to the v_t when she's sick.

20. I have tw_ arms.

21. My birthday cake had c_ndles.

22. There are s_lt and pepper shakers on my counter.

23. My mom plays t_nnis.

24. The y_rn is soft.

25. V_lcanos spew lava.

26. The sk_ is full of clouds.

27. Rac_cars are fast.

28. I like classical m_sic.

29. The c_t is friendly.

30. The b_rd flies fast.

Activity Three: Circle That Word!

In each group, find the words that start with a vowel and circle them! Remember, the vowels are a, e, i, o, u, so if the word starts with a, e, i, o, or u, then it starts with a vowel!

Group 1) Unicycle, bike, helmet

Group 2) Halloween, Christmas, Easter

Group 3) Undershirt, sweater, hat

Group 4) Astronaut, spaceship, planet

Group 5) Uncle, cousin, grandparent

Group 6) Monkey, ape, forest

Group 7) Clown, circus, balloon

Group 8) Mouse, elephant, fish

Group 9) Water, earth, fire

Group 10) White, blue, orange

Group 11) Leg, hand, ear

Group 12) Snow, cold, igloo

Group 13) Hawk, owl, crow

Group 14) Sun, fire, ice

Group 15) Cake, brownie, ice cream

Group 16) Train, car, airplane

Group 17) Potato, onion, turnip

Group 18) Child, baby, infant

Group 19) Lizard, tree, iguana

Group 20) Pencil, eraser, paper

Group 21) Otter, fish, river

Group 22) Circle, square, oval

Group 23) Boat, water, oar

Group 24) Whale, dolphin, orca

Group 25) Orange, banana, pear

Group 26) Pickle, olive, carrot

Group 27) Burger, sandwich, egg salad

Group 28) Lake, river, ocean

Group 29) Owl, barn, rafters

Group 30) Square, hexagon, octagon

Activity Four: Write That Word!

The following words start with vowels, which are the letters a, e, i, o, u. Trace them out to write them yourself!

Group 1) Umbrella _____

Group 2) Oar ___

Group 3) Elephant _____

Group 4) Astronaut _____

Group 5) Owl ___

Group 6) Arm ___

Group 7) Acorn _____

Group 8) Apple _____

Group 9) Igloo _____

Group 10) Octopus _____

Group 11) Uniform _____

Group 12) Anchor _____

Group 13) Aunt ____

Group 14) Uncle _____

Group 15) Eyes ____

Group 16) Ears ____

Group 17) Ant ___

Group 18) Ice ___

Group 19) Old ___

Group 20) Umpire _____

Group 21) Air ___

Group 22) Eel ___

Group 23) Ice Cream _____

Group 24) Otter _____

Group 25) Ugly ____

Group 26) Art ___

Group 27) Eat ___

Group 28) Ick ___

Group 29) Up __

Group 30) Elf ___

Activity Five: Find The Missing Word!

Find the missing word from each sentence. Hint: it's a word that starts with a vowel! Remember, the vowels are a, e, i, o, u.

Group 1) The boat needs an ____. (Anchor, banana, scissors.)

Group 2) Chickens lay ___. (Squirrels, juice boxes, eggs.)

Group 3) My favorite cold treat is _____. (Apples, ice cream, sand.)

Group 4) I love eating _____. (Milk, apples, steak.)

Group 5) _____ live in the ocean. (Butterflies, elephants, octopus.)

Group 6) The pencil has an _____. (Concrete, eraser, bag.)

Group 7) My arm bends at the ____. (Leg, hand, elbow.)

Group 8) I have a great ___! (Sandal, bell, idea.)

Group 9) _____ are pretend. (Unicorns, walls, elephants.)

Group 10) He shot an _____. (Leg, bottle, arrow.)

Group 11) I love visiting the ____. (Sky, ocean, phone.)

Group 12) ___ live in ant hills. (Birds, ants, butterflies.)

Group 13) _____ are big mammals! (Fish, monkeys, elephants.)

Group 14) ___ is kept in the freezer. (Knife, tack, ice.)

Group 15) I use an _____ to stay dry in the rain. (Floor, umbrella, sky.)

Group 16) The train uses a steam ____. (Boat, machine, engine.)

Group 17) He flew there by _____. (Bus, train, airplane.)

Group 18) We have gone on vacation to the _____. (Mall, island, grocery store.)

Group 19) My favorite bird is an _____. (Crow, eagle, bat.)

Group 20) She cut the wood with an ___. (Knife, axe, scissors.)

Group 21) He played a song on the _____. (Car, accordion, bat.)

Group 22) Carrots are _____. (Flat, orange, soft.)

Group 23) Big kids wear _____. (Orange, underwear, roof.)

Group 24) The ___ says "hoot!" (Owl, fish, water.)

Group 25) They sent the mail in an _____. (Bag, truck, envelope.)

Group 26) A spider is a type of _____. (Bird, insect, mammal.)

Group 27) Squirrels like to eat ____. (Frogs, acorns, trees.)

Group 28) The barn had an ___. (Owl, pickle, fish.)

Group 29) The pen draws using ___. (Ink, mud, paint.)

Group 30) Grandpa likes to sit in his _____. (Ground, room, armchair.)

Activity Six: Spell The Word!

These words start with vowels! Remember, the vowels are a, e, i, o, u. Sound these words out out, then write them yourself next to the original word.

1. Ant   2. Egg   3. Owl   4. Ear   5. Eye   6. Arm   7. Oar   8. Oat

9. Ask   10. Eel   11. Ice   12. Ugly   13. Art   14. Etch   15. Itch

16. Ouch   17. And   18. Aunt   19. Eat   20. Ear   21. Ice   22. Owl

23. Urn   24. Eye   25. Ewe   26. Ick   27. Ink   28. Old   29. Out

30. Ash

Activity Seven: Draw A Picture!

The bold word will represent either a consonant or a vowel. Color over it in red if it is a consonant, or blue if it is a vowel. Remember, the vowels are: a, e, i, o, u. If the word does not start with a, e, i, o, or u, then it starts with a consonant.

1. A red **owl**.

2. A **blue** fish.

3. The fat **cat**.

4. Cold **ice cream** cone.

5. **The** yellow pen.

6. An **orange** and a banana.

7. The little **jar**.

8. **My** hand is full.

9. The bee lives **in** the hive.

10. Let's go have **some** fun in the sun.

11. The pot is **old**.

12. I like to eat burgers **and** fries.

13. My **frog** likes to jump.

14. The cat has pink **lips**.

15. The **beach** is sandy.

16. She has pretty **hair**.

17. He **is** always running.

18. The cat **likes** to sleep.

19. **I** love the sunshine.

20. He has a thick **beard**.

21. The **egg** was scrambled.

22. Birds are my **favorite**.

23. The moon rises **at** night.

24. The **shop** sells good candy.

25. I fly my kite **at** the park.

26. My brother likes to **play** with trucks.

27. I **eat** fresh strawberry jam.

28. The garden is **my** favorite place.

29. The fish swims in the **ocean**.

30. Trees blow **in** the wind.

Chapter 4: Phonemes

Phenomes are the sounds of the letters you are using. For example, "a" sounds like "aye" or "ah" depending on how you say it. Learning about the different phenomes helps you sound out letters so that you can learn to spell!

Activity One: What Is The Difference?

The following words have just one different letter! See if you can sound each one out and identify what it means!

Group 1) Bat and Bad

Group 2) Cat and Can

Group 3) Tag and Tan

Group 4) Jam and Jar

Group 5) Vat and Van

Group 6) Bet and Beg

Group 7) Rat and Ran

Group 8) Ham and Hat

Group 9) Mat and Map

Group 10) Fat and Fan

Group 11) Ran and Rap

Group 12) Pen and Pet

Group 13) Leg and Let

Group 14) Pet and Peg

Group 15) Men and Met

Group 16) Nap and Nab

Group 17) Bag and Bat

Group 18) Mat and Man

Group 19) Tap and Tan

Group 20) Mad and Map

Group 21) Bed and Bet

Group 22) Peg and Pen

Group 23) Log and Lot

Group 24) Toy and Ton

Group 25) Sow and Son

Group 26) Fox and Fog

Group 27) Hot and Hog

Group 28) His and Hit

Group 29) Mow and Mom

Group 30) Lip and Lid

Activity Two: Sound And Write

Sound out the following words and then write them down next to the original word.

1. C – A – T

2. C – A – N

3. C – A – P

4. B – A – G

5. D – A – M

6. D – A – D

7. H – A – S

8. D – E – N

9. J – E – T

10. K – E – G

11. B – A – T

12. F – A – N

13. L – A – P

14. R – A – G

15. J – A – M

16. L – A – D

17. W – A – S

18. H – E – N

19. N – E – T

20. L – E – G

21. R – E – D

22. H – A – T

23. M – A – N

24. M – A – P

25. T – A – G

26. R – A – M

27. P – A – D

28. M – E – N

29. P – E – T

30. P – E – G

Activity Three: Sound Out These Words

Practice reading by sounding the following words out using the alphabet you learned above!

Three Letter Words:

- Bat
- Can
- Cat
- Cub
- Cut
- Day
- Den
- Dog
- Fit
- Fog
- Fun
- Hit
- Log
- Map
- May
- Met
- Mow
- Nod
- Pad
- Pay

- Pen
- Rod
- Sad
- Say
- Sun
- Tap
- Van
- Way
- Yet
- Zed

Activity Four: Fill In The Missing Word

Fill in the missing word from the following sentences.

1. The pen writes with ___ ink. (Red, mud, sky.)

2. The rain makes everything ___. (Blue, wet, sand.)

3. I can count all the way to ___. (Air, otter, ten.)

4. There is a ___ by the door. (Mat, tree, fish.)

5. I enjoy ___ dinner. (Mom, dad, ham.)

6. I like to ___ my dog. (Fish, pet, wet.)

7. My favorite color is ___. (Blue, fish, sky.)

8. I sleep in my ___ at night. (Car, fly, bed.)

9. The ___ lays eggs in a nest. (Hen, tree, cat.)

10. I clean my mess with a ___. (Boat, rag, blanket.)

11. I believe I ___. (Can, bed, closet.)

12. Tighten the ___ on the milk, please! (Lid, door, bird.)

13. You can get there with the ___. (Dog, map, hat.)

14. I like ___ on my toast. (Jam, nail, bat.)

15. I yell when I am ___. (Fish, mad, boat.)

16. My cat sits in my ___. (Lap, hat, tree.)

17. The ___ ate the cheese. (Lamp, rat, fish.)

18. I can ___ you! (See, hat, pet.)

19. The ___ played ball. (Boy, wall, toy.)

20. I wear my ___ when it is hot outside. (Ball, hat, pen.)

21. The teacher asked me to ___. (Tin, sit, mow.)

22. The dog licked it's ___. (Rot, bat, lip.)

23. I drink from a ___. (Ham, cup, fox.)

24. The rain made me ___. (Boy, dam, wet.)

25. The ___ sleeps upside down. (Hat, mat, bat.)

26. I watched an ___ carry a leaf. (Tan, ant, bag.)

27. Water comes from the ___. (Sap, mat, tap.)

28. I really want to ___! (Van, win, lap.)

29. The dog ___ her tail. (Wags, fat, bags.)

30. I like to ___. (Bag, cap, jog.)

Activity Five: Draw A Picture

Read the following words out loud. Then, draw a picture of them!

1. Hat	2. Cup	3. Fox	4. Bat	5. Sit
6. Box	7. Lip	8. Ham	9. Boy	10. Run
11. Man	12. Toy	13. Mow	14. Jam	15. Jar
16. Mat	17. Rat	18. Map	19. Van	20. Rag
21. Dog	22. Cat	23. Pen	24. Mug	25. Bed
26. Fog	27. Two	28. Dot	29. Egg	30. Cow

Activity Six: Spot The Missing Letter

Find the missing letter in each of the words below, then write it in!

1. Dog, log, h_g.

2. Set, l_t, get.

3. Pig, big, r_g.

4. F_n, pin, win.

5. Ran, f_n, van.

6. W_t, get, let.

7. M_g, jug, rug.

8. Hen, p_n, ten.

9. H_d, mad, bad.

10. Lip, sip, h_p.

11. Pit, s_t, hit.

12. S_n, fun, run.

13. Log, dog, b_g.

14. Pad, b_d, sad.

15. Mow, s_w, row.

16. M_p, lap, yap.

17. Fan, p_n, can.

18. Rod, sod, n_d.

19. Rug, bug, d_g.

20. Bag, r_g, nag.

21. Pig, r_g, dig.

22. M_p, cap, lap.

23. Win, p_n, fin.

24. Hop, mop, t_p.

25. Set, l_t, get.

26. R_g, mug, bug.

27. Mat, pat, f_t.

28. Can, tan, v_n.

29. Map, tap, l_p.

30. Red, bed, T_d.

Chapter 5: Rhyming

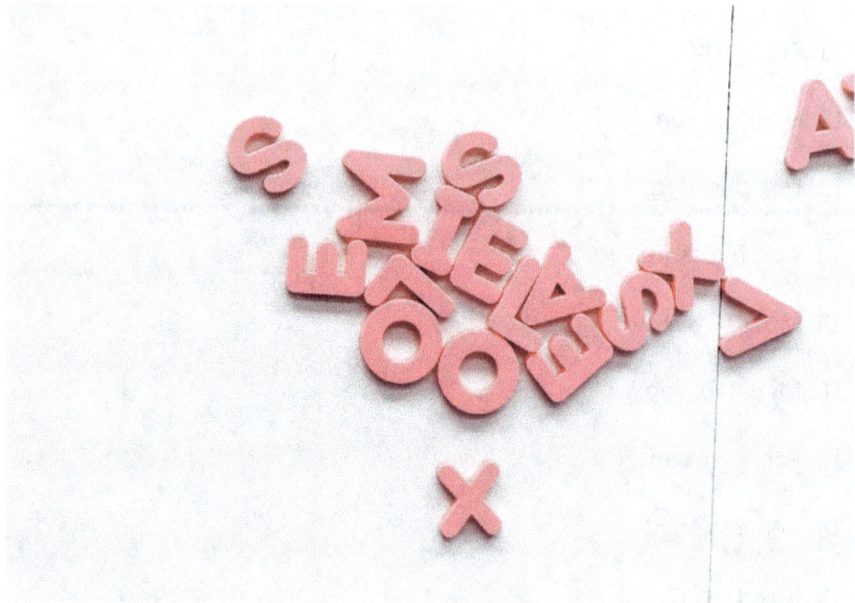

When two words end with the same sound, that is called a rhyme. For example, b*at* and c*at*, are rhyming words. C*at* and ca*p*, or ba*t* and ba*g* are not rhyming words. The words must sound the same at the end if they are true rhyming words. Rhymes are used to make all sorts of fun things in the world, like music and poetry. See what words you can rhyme!

<u>Activity One: Do They Rhyme?</u>

Below you will find two words side by side. Give them a check mark if they rhyme, or an "X" if they don't.

Group 1) Bat and Hat

Group 2) Cat and Rat

Group 3) Tie and Tip

Group 4) Sip and Sit

Group 5) Mad and Bad

Group 6) Hen and Pen

Group 7) Wet and Let

Group 8) Mug and Mud

Group 9) Pig and Pit

Group 10) Had and Dad

Group 11) Son and Mom

Group 12) Met and Pet

Group 13) Fog and Bog

Group 14) Egg and Eat

Group 15) Fly and Sky

Group 16) Far and Car

Group 17) For and Fog

Group 18) Eye and Ear

Group 19) Jet and Net

Group 20) Bet and Bat

Group 21) Has and Hat

Group 22) Lad and Mad

Group 23) Tag and Tap

Group 24) Rag and Bag

Group 25) Lap and Map

Group 26) Pan and Pen

Group 27) Peg and Leg

Group 28) Bed and Red

Group 29) Rat and Fat

Group 30) Rat and Rag

Activity Two: Match The Rhyming Words

In the following groups of words, two out of the five words rhyme. Can you find them and match them together?

Group 1) Bat, pan, rap, lam, hat

Group 2) Tag, jam, pad, man, rag

Group 3) Men, ram, pad, pen, van

Group 4) Met, ten, mad, ham, pen

Group 5) Leg, red, lad, was, bed

Group 6) Map, ram, rag, rat, bag

Group 7) Ten, bet, tap, pan, rap

Group 8) Den, bet, lam, red, hen

Group 9) Nap, pan, tag, tap, lam

Group 10) Bet, ten, pad, map, mad

Group 11) Mat, rap, fat, mad, was

Group 12) Peg, jet, leg, has, pad

Group 13) Dad, bet, ten, ban, fan

Group 14) Tag, hat, can, pan, men

Group 15) Bet, wet, mad, ham, pan

Group 16) Bed, net, hen, red, tap

Group 17) Met, mad, map, mat, bet

Group 18) Peg, hen, lad, nap, leg

Group 19) Ten, ham, tag, wet, rag

Group 20) Pan, tag, mad, men, pad

Group 21) Wet, ham, rap, vet, red

Group 22) Hen, pad, men, let, red

Group 23) Rap, tag, fan, lap, wet

Group 24) Peg, ram, nap, lam, ten

Group 25) Bet, let, map, man, mat

Group 26) Peg, pet, pen, pan, van

Group 27) Mad, ram, pet, bet, tap

Group 28) Lam, mad, pan, fat, rat

Group 29) Met, ham, vet, peg, red

Group 30) Yam, mad, bet, rap, pad

Activity Three: Find A Rhyming Word

Find a word that rhymes with each of the following words!

1. Bat and ___.

2. Car and ___.

3. Cut and ___.

4. May and ___.

5. Pet and ___.

6. Cat and ___.

7. Dog and ___.

8. Fly and ___.

9. Say and ___.

10. Box and ___.

11. Can and ___.

12. Pen and ___.

13. Cup and ___.

14. Let and ___.

15. Rat and ___.

16. Far and ___.

17. But and ___.

18. Say and ___.

19. Bet and ___.

20. Hat and ___.

21. Sky and ___.

22. Pan and ___.

23. Fox and ___.

24. Mom and ___.

25. Dad and ___.

26. Sad and ___.

27. Hum and ___.

28. Top and ___.

29. Saw and ___.

30. Rag and ___.

Activity Four: Write The Rhyme

The following words are groups of rhyming words. Read them, spell them out, and then practice writing them down on your own!

Group 1) Bat and Hat. _____

Group 2) Cut and Put. _____

Group 3) New and Two. _____

Group 4) Bad and Sad. _____

Group 5) Dog and Log. _____

Group 6) Not and Hot. _____

Group 7) Big and Pig. _____

Group 8) Cup and Pup. _____

Group 9) Car and Far. _____

Group 10) Rat and Cat. _____

Group 11) Bet and Let. _____

Group 12) Can and Pan. _____

Group 13) Pen and Hen. _____

Group 14) Dry and Try. _____

Group 15) Day and Say. _____

Group 16) Hot and Pot. _____

Group 17) May and Say. _____

Group 18) Pet and Set. _____

Group 19) Red and Bed. _____

Group 20) Sit and Pit. _____

Group 21) Way and Day. _____

Group 22) You and Two. _____

Group 23) Man and Pan. _____

Group 24) Get and Let. _____

Group 25) Mat and Cat. _____

Group 26) Nut and Hut. _____

Group 27) Mug and Bug. _____

Group 28) Ten and Hen. _____

Group 29) Jog and Log. _____

Group 30) Hop and Mop. _____

Activity Five: Do They Rhyme?

These rhyme words are a little harder than the last. Can you sound them out and figure out if they rhyme or not?

Group 1) Book and Took

Group 2) Fine and Dash

Group 3) Wipe and Pipe

Group 4) Fall and Wave

Group 5) Wail and Sail

Group 6) Dine and Fine

Group 7) Same and Call

Group 8) Save and Wave

Group 9) Cash and Dash

Group 10) Lame and Same

Group 11) Cook and Walk

Group 12) Meet and Feet

Group 13) Fall and Call

Group 14) Hall and Ball

Group 15) Took and Meet

Group 16) Cook and Took

Group 17) Jail and Pack

Group 18) Same and Fame

Group 19) Sack and Rack

Group 20) Fake and Take

Group 21) Pack and Sack

Group 22) Jail and Fail

Group 23) Slap and Clap

Group 24) Cake and Take

Group 25) Lock and Lake

Group 26) Sole and Role

Group 27) Fish and Dish

Group 28) Tail and Come

Group 29) Fame and Save

Group 30) Come and Some

Activity Six: Draw A Picture!

Read the following rhymes, then draw a picture of what you have read!

Group 1) The *bat* is playing with the *cat*.

Group 2) The *fish* ate off of a *dish*.

Group 3) The *cat* is wearing a *hat*.

Group 4) The *pig* is really *BIG*!

Group 5) The *mug* was sitting on the *rug*.

Group 6) The *dog* was jumping over a *log*.

Group 7) The *van* had a really large *fan*.

Group 8) The *bug* drank from a *mug*.

Group 9) The *hen* wrote with a *pen*.

Group 10) The *map* was on his *lap*.

Group 11) He put the cup to his *lip* to take a *sip*.

Group 12) The *cat* laid on the *mat*.

Group 13) The *frog* slept on a *log*.

Group 14) We had *fun* on a nice long *run*.

Group 15) My fish was a very *wet pet*.

Group 16) The *fox* slept in a small *box*.

Group 17) The *rat* liked to be *pat*.

Group 18) My *pet* road on a *jet*.

Group 19) The *hen* could count to *ten*.

Group 20) The *egg* had its very own *leg*!

Group 21) I liked to put *jam* on my *ham*.

Group 22) As *snug* as a *bug* in a *rug*.

Group 23) The *bat* liked to play with the *rat*.

Group 24) I washed my *cub* in the *tub*.

Group 25) The fish was a *tin* with a *fin*.

Group 26) He lived in a *nut* shaped *hut*.

Group 27) The friendly *cow* took a *bow*.

Group 28) The *dog* went for a long *jog*.

Group 29) The *bat* wore a funny shaped *hat*.

Group 30) There was a *den* made just for the *hen*.

PART II

Chapter 1: Ricky Responsibility

Ricky Responsibility was a hero of responsibility. His number one mission in life was to teach children everywhere about the importance of responsibility.

Ricky Responsibility taught children to wash their clothes, their toes, and their nose. He taught children to put away their toys and to be kind to all the girls and boys. Ricky always wanted to see children be good and do the things they knew they should.

Whether it is learning right from wrong, or cleaning their rooms after a day so long, Ricky Responsibility wants to see every kid make the right choice.

Learning to take responsibility for yourself, and to fulfill your responsibilities in life is not always easy. Ricky Responsibility knows that, so he teaches his friends three important rules.

The first rule Ricky Responsibility teaches is the rule of *getting the job done*. No matter how hard it may be, you are the one to get the job done, and the job *must* get done! Whether it's helping your Mom buy groceries or helping your Dad mow the lawn, there is always something that needs to be done. Doing your part to get it done means the job is a lot easier for everyone!

The second rule Ricky Responsibility teaches is the rule of being thoughtful. Your actions always affect others, and you want your actions to help others, not hurt them. By being thoughtful, you make the world a wonderful place for everyone around you, so they can enjoy being around you, too!

The third rule Ricky Responsibility teaches is the rule of owning your actions. You must own all of the actions you take, whether they are good, bad, or a mistake. Since you have chosen them, they are your actions to own up to, and that is exactly what you should do. When you own the actions you take, you can fix your mistakes, learn right from wrong, and do better than you have ever done!

When you take responsibility for yourself, everyone cheers! You may even hear the cheers of Ricky Responsibility himself, as he cheers you on for becoming your best self!

Chapter 2: Hannah Learns About Hard Work

Working hard may not always seem fun, but it is an important way to get your work done. Hannah learned a great deal about hard work when her grandpa came over to help her dad build a new shed in the backyard. Hannah's mom needed a shed for her garden tools, and her dad wanted to keep his lawnmower in there, too. Hannah's dad even told her that once the shed was built, she could store her bike in the shed, too! She really wanted a place to store her bike that would be very special for herself.

When Hannah's grandpa got there, Hannah was determined to help build the shed so that they could build it as fast as possible. After all, the sooner the shed was built, the sooner Hannah would have a place for her bike!

First, Hannah helped her grandpa and dad collect the tools they needed to build the shed. They went to the hardware store and bought boards, nails, and a door for the shed. Then, they went home and unloaded the tools into the backyard so they could get ready to build the shed together.

When all of the tools were in the backyard, Hannah helped her grandpa and dad read the blueprint or the plans for how to build the shed. Then, they laid all of the wood out to show where each board would be hammered into place. Hannah helped her grandpa and dad carry the wood, lay it out, and then she helped them hold it in place so they could hammer the boards together.

Once most of the boards were in place, Hannah's dad even let her hammer some of them together! She fixed boards where they belonged, hammered nails into place, and made sure that she built the shed nice and sturdy so all of her mom's garden tools, her dad's lawnmower, and her bike would have somewhere to stay.

After all of the boards were in place, Hannah, her grandpa, and her dad cut a hole for the door and fixed the door into place, too. They tested it to make sure it worked by swinging the door open and closed. Hannah ran inside, closed the door, and then opened the door and popped back out. "Do you see me?!" She asked, giggling from behind the door. "We see you!" her dad and grandpa said, smiling back.

When they were all done, Hannah helped her mom put her garden tools in the new shed. Then, she helped her dad roll the lawnmower in and place it in the corner where it would stay from now on. Finally, Hannah rode her bike into the shed and set it up in its very own spot. She put her helmet on the handlebars and smiled, pleased with the new parking spot she had built for her bike with the help of her grandpa and her dad.

Chapter 3: Chester Gains His Confidence!

Chester could be very scared. Anytime he had to try something new, Chester would feel fear growing inside of him. He would worry about what he had to do, what others would be doing, and about what he did not know.

One day, Chester's mom signed him up for a field trip at school. He was going to be going to the aquarium with his friends! He knew it would be a lot of fun, but Chester could not help but feel scared. He worried about the bus ride there, all the new people, and all the new things he would see. Chester worried he would get lost, that all of the new people would overwhelm him, or that he would see a scary fish at the aquarium.

As they got on the bus, Chester's teacher noticed he was scared. "Are you ok?" His teacher asked. "No! I'm scared!" Chester said. "Why?" His teacher asked. "What if I don't like it? Or I see something scary? What if I get lost!" He said. "I understand, Chester. I would be scared, too, if I saw something scary or got lost. But you will not see anything scary, and you will not get lost. And I know you will like our trip to the aquarium!" His teacher said. "What if I don't?" Chester whined. "You will." His teacher said.

Chester climbed on the bus, still worried about how he felt. He walked all the way to the middle of the bus and sat down next to his friend Tomas. "What's wrong?" Tomas asked. "I'm scared," Chester said. "Why are you scared?" Tomas asked. "Because I've never been to the aquarium before!" Chester whined. "Me neither. I'm so excited!" Tomas said. Chester looked at Tomas, eyes wide with shock. "Really? You are excited?" Chester asked. "Yes! I want to see a big whale!" Tomas smiled. "Oh, that would be fun!" Chester agreed. "Yes! And I want to see the gift shop! I want to buy a shark! My mom gave me money." Tomas smiled. Chester thought about the money his mom gave him earlier that morning. "Well, that would be fun." Chester agreed.

Chester looked out the window as they drove to the aquarium. When he got there, Chester jumped out of his seat, feeling a little more excited. For a moment, he was scared by all of the new sights and people. Then, Chester remembered how Tomas said he was excited to see a whale and to buy a new shark. Chester wanted to do those things, too! He started to feel excited.

As Chester walked through the gates into the aquarium, he felt his confidence growing. He knew he was going to have fun with his friend Tomas! For the rest of the day, Chester practiced being confident. By the time they were leaving the aquarium, he was very sad because he was having so much fun!

Chester was surprised that being confident made him have so much more fun than he did when he was scared. Chester decided from then on that he would be confident about new experiences, even if he did feel a little scared sometimes.

Chapter 4: Carly Learns to Communicate

Carly was excited to start school with her friends. She had already been to preschool and kindergarten, so Carly knew what going back to school was like. She was excited about making a name tag, introducing herself to her teacher, and making new friends. She was especially excited about gym class because now Carly was old enough to play soccer with the other kids!

When she arrived at school on the first day, Carly noticed things were very different. This year, her friends were not sitting at circle tables with coloring pencils in the middle. Instead, they were sitting at small desks, all pointed to the front of the room, and they had no coloring pencils on them. In fact, they didn't have anything on them.

When class started, things were different. They did not stand in a circle and introduce themselves. Instead, they each stood next to their desk and said hello, said three things about themselves, then sat down. There was not much time for coloring because they had learning to do. They didn't even have a story circle on the first day. Things were very different from preschool and kindergarten.

At the end of the day, Carly was feeling sad and angry because the day did not go the way she wanted it to. Carly missed kindergarten. When her dad came to pick her up, instead of being kind, Carly was rude. She threw her bag in the car, jumped into her seat, kicked the seat in front of her, and ignored her dad. Carly's dad knew something was wrong, but he did not know *what* was wrong. Because he did not know what was wrong, Carly's dad could not help her. Carly stayed angry and had no one to help her feel better.

When they got home, Carly was still angry. She ran in the house, slammed the door behind her, and ran up to her room, and slammed that door, too. Now, Carly's dad was upset with her behavior. He wanted her to tell him what was wrong, but instead, she was not nice to him.

Carly's dad followed her up to her room, sat down at her desk, and asked her what was wrong. Finally, Carly told him. "School was not fun! I miss kindergarten!" she said. "Why?" her dad asked. "Because we sat with our friends and colored! Today, we did not sit with our friends or color! We did not even get storytime!" Carly cried. "I understand. That sounds very different from before." Her dad said, giving her a hug. "Thank you for telling me why you are so angry. Now, I know how to help you feel better. Before you did not tell me, so I did not know how to help you. How about we go color pictures together?" Her dad asked. "Yes please!" Carly said, hopping off the bed and running to color a picture with her dad, who happened to be one of her very best friends.

Chapter 5: Lester Learns a Lesson About Love

Lester was only six years old when he learned a lesson about love.

Lester knew that he loved his mom and dad, his little sister, and his dog, too. He also knew he loved his dinosaur toy and his bike, and his best friend, Jason.

When Lester thought about love, he thought about all the happy memories he had with his favorite people and toys. He thought about the time his friend came on a road trip with his family, and they brought their toy dinosaurs. He thought about the time he went fishing with his dad, and the time his mom taught him to bake muffins. Lester also thought about the time his best friend invited him for a sleepover, and they watched movies all night. When Lester thought about love, he thought about happy memories.

One day, Lester was tired after school. He sat down on the couch and relaxed, instead of putting his things away like his mom asked. Lester's mom asked him to clean up his things, but Lester did not listen. She asked one more time, then she turned off the TV and told him to go to his room.

"You do not love me!" Lester cried, running away. "That is not true." His mom said. "You do not love me! You are making me clean when I am tired!" He said again. "Lester, I am tired too, and these are not my things. I love you very much, but this is not my responsibility. You need to clean up your own belongings." His mom said. "I don't want to!" He cried. "I don't want to, either." His mom said. "You're mean! You make me do things I don't want to!" Lester said.

"Lester, I am tired, too. I still have my own things to do. How about this, would you like to clean the dishes, walk the dog, and mow the lawn so I can clean up your belongings?" His mom asked. Lester thought about it for a moment. "No." He said. "Exactly. Cleaning your things is your chore, and the other things are mine. I love you, but you need to respect me." His mom said. "I understand," Lester said as he went to clean up his things.

Lester thought about it as he cleaned up. He realized now that loving someone did not always mean happy memories and doing fun things together. Loving someone also meant respecting them and being kind to them. From then on, Lester was always respectful and kind to the people he loved.

Chapter 6: Felicia Spends Time With Family

Felicia loved spending time with her family. Most days, Felicia spent her family time with her parents and her two younger sisters. Sometimes, they would go to Felicia's grandparent's house, and they would spend time together with even more family. Felicia's aunt, uncles, and all of her cousins would come, too.

Felicia loved it when the whole family got together because it was always so much fun. She and her cousins would play in the backyard, her aunt and uncles would always have water gun fights with them, and her grandma and grandpa always made good food. Grandma made the best casseroles, and grandpa made the best pies.

Today, Felicia and her mom and dad and two sisters were going to be going over to her grandparent's house. She was so excited! She packed up all her things, put them in her bag, and got ready to leave. At exactly 11 in the morning, they packed up into the car and drove to grandma and grandpa's house. They got there shortly after 12.

Just as Felicia hoped, all of her family was there. She ran to say hello to her grandma, grandpa, aunt, two uncles, and nine cousins. Once they put their things down, Felicia and her cousins ran into the yard to play with their water guns. Felicia's aunt and uncles came out back and started playing, filling the water guns and spraying them all with the big soaker guns. Felicia's mom and dad joined, too, and at one point, her grandma and grandpa even started playing!

When it got later, Felicia's grandma brought out a fresh salad she had made. The salad was so yummy. Then, Felicia's grandpa started barbecuing burgers. They ate their barbecued burgers and ate delicious pie for dessert. After they ate, her whole family went for a walk to a nearby park, and Felicia played on the playground with her sisters and cousins.

Later that night, Felicia and her family packed their things. Felicia, her mom and dad and both sisters all drove back home. On the way home, her parents asked if they had a good time. "I did! I love visiting family." Felicia smiled. "Me too!" her sisters said at the same time.

Chapter 7: Sean Gets Sick

Sean was sitting in his desk at school when, suddenly, he started feeling unwell. Sean felt hot, and his stomach was churning. He could feel himself getting more tired, so he laid his head down on his desk. "Are you ok, Sean?" his teacher asked. "No, I feel sick!" Sean said. "Oh no! We should call your parents. It is important to go home and relax when you are sick." His teacher said. "But I don't want to go home! I want to play with my friends!" Sean said. "I know. You can come back when you are feeling better. Your parents will come get you now." Sean's teacher said.

Sean really wanted to stay with his friends but agreed that it was important to get well first.

Sean's dad picked him up from school and brought him home. When they got home, Sean's dad helped him lie in bed and relax so he could start to feel better. "I don't want to relax; I want to play!" Sean whined. "I know, Sean. But you have to relax when you are sick. It helps you feel better when you have been sick." His dad said. "Will I feel better soon?" Sean asked. "Yes." His dad said.

Sean laid in bed. His head felt warm, his nose felt stuffed, and his belly felt sick. Every time he rolled over, he winced as the pain got worse before it got better. After a while of just lying there, Sean finally fell asleep.

When he fell asleep, Sean dreamed about being at school with his friends. He dreamt about playing with the push cars, swinging on the swings, and going down the slide. Sean dreamt about having lunch with his friends, learning about the alphabet, and coloring in his favorite coloring book. He dreamt about everything he loved, which was many things because Sean really loved going to school.

Eventually, Sean woke up from his nap. When he did, his dad and mom were in the room with him. "How are you feeling?" his mom asked, resting the back of her hand on Sean's forehead. "Ok," Sean said. The cool touch of his mom's hand felt good against his forehead, which felt warm because of the fever he had from his sickness. "You still feel warm." She frowned. "I know." He sighed.

Sean's dad brought him a cup of water. Then, his mom brought him some chicken noodle soup. Sean drank the water and ate the soup, then laid back down against his pillow. Although he was still feeling sick, Sean started to feel some relief from his symptoms.

When his mom and dad left the room, Sean laid back down and rested his head against his pillow. Once again, he slept. This time, Sean dreamt about watching TV, climbing trees, and playing with his dog, Pal. Sean loved dreaming about wonderful things that made him happy.

It wasn't until the next morning when Sean woke up. His sickness had made him so tired that he slept all the way through dinner, and through the entire night! By morning, Sean was starting to feel much better. His fever was gone, his nose was clear, and his belly was almost all better.

"How are you feeling this morning?" His dad asked while his mom prepared their lunches. "A lot better, but my belly still hurts," Sean responded. "Do you feel good enough to go to school?" His dad asked. "No, but this time I will not be sad about it because I know how important it is to take care of myself. Tomorrow, I will be feeling completely better. I'm sure of it!" Sean said. "Sounds good." His mom smiled.

Sean spent the rest of the day lying in bed, working on feeling better. As the day went on, his tummy started to feel better. By the next morning, Sean was feeling completely better and ready to go back to school. So, he did! When he got there, he was so happy to be with his friends again, and to know that he had taken such good care of himself that he had plenty of energy to push cars, play on the swings, and go down the slides with his friends. It was a good day!

Chapter 8: Melissa Makes a New Friend

Melissa always played with her friends Kayla and Beth. Kayla and Beth lived on the other side of town, but their moms were friends, so they always got together to do fun things. When it was time for school to start, Melissa got nervous. Kayla and Beth would be going to the same school, but Melissa would be going to a different school where she knew no one.

The day before school started, Melissa's mom found her in her room crying. "What is the matter?" Her mom asked. "I will not have any friends at school. I do not want to go!" Melissa cried, worried that school would be scary with no friends. "That is why you are going to school to make new friends." Her mom smiled. "I don't want new friends. I like Kayla and Beth!" Melissa pouted. "Kayla and Beth are wonderful friends. It is good to have many friends, though, Melissa." Her mom said, hugging her. "I don't want many friends." Melissa kept crying. Melissa's mom hugged her close and thought about what to say.

"When I first started school, I was afraid, too." Her mom said. "You were?" Melissa asked. "Oh, yes! I worried no one would like me, and I would have no one to play with. I did not have friends like Kayla and Beth; either, I was all by myself." Her mom said. "That is said," Melissa said, crying still. "It was, but I made many wonderful friends at school. I did not believe my mom when she said I would, but I did! In fact, that is how I met Kayla and Beth's mom, and now we are still friends!" Her mom said. "Really?" Melissa asked, her eyes growing wide. "Really." Her mom smiled. "If you did not go to school, you would not have met her?" Melissa asked. "No." Her mom replied.

Melissa stopped and thought for a while. She watched the clouds go by as she thought about what school would be like. She wondered who she would meet, what they would be like, and if she would like any of them. Melissa wondered if she would have fun and if school wouldn't be so bad after all. Then, she wondered about what Kayla and Beth were going to do on their first day of school. She thought about how they, too, would be going into new classrooms, making new friends, and having fun. Melissa thought that if Kayla and Beth could do it, surely she could do it, too.

The next day, Melissa got up and got ready for school. She got dressed, brushed her teeth and her hair, ate breakfast, and laced up her shoes the way her dad had taught her. When the time was right, she grabbed her backpack and walked to the car with her mom. On the way to school, Melissa quietly thought about what the first day would be like. "Are you excited?" Her mom asked when they were almost there. "Yes." Melissa said, folding her hands in her lap. "Will you make new friends?" Her mom asked. "Yes." Melissa said, wondering if that was true.

When she arrived at school, Melissa felt afraid, but she knew that her friends would not want her to be scared. So, she bravely went inside and started getting to know new people. She started by introducing herself to her teacher. Then, she introduced herself to the people sitting near her. When class started, her teacher had everyone sit in a circle, and they all introduced themselves to each other. Melissa thought two of the girls in her class might make for wonderful friends. Their names were Ashley and Shupe.

At recess, Melissa introduced herself to Ashley and Shupe. The three of them got along really well and spent the entire time playing tag and talking about how excited they were for school to be starting. By the time recess was over, Melissa knew she had made two wonderful new friends.

When school ended, Melissa's mom picked her up. On the way home, her mom asked, "So, did you make any new friends?" "I did!" Melissa smiled. "Oh? Who are they?" Her mom asked. "Ashley and Shupe. They are in my class! We played tag at recess. I am excited to see them again tomorrow." Melissa said. "That is wonderful. I knew you would make friends! All you had to do was be brave, and try your best, and it worked!" Her mom smiled. "That's right!" Melissa smiled back.

Every day for the rest of the year, Melissa enjoyed playing with her friends Ashley and Shupe, and she also enjoyed playing with her friends Kayla and Beth. On her birthday, her mom even invited them all over, and they all played together and had great fun. Melissa realized she loved making friends and hoped she would make even more the next school year.

Chapter 9: Austin Learns to Care for Animals

Austin was six years old when his parents bought him his very own puppy. Radar, the brown Labrador retriever, was a friendly little fluffy puppy. He loved to lick hands, do tricks for treats, and go for walks with Austin and his parents. Although it was fun to get a new puppy, Austin realized they came with a lot of responsibility. That meant that Austin had to do a lot of work to take care of his little puppy, Radar!

Every morning, Austin had to clean the food and water dishes and give Radar fresh food and water. He would then take Radar into the backyard so the puppy could go to the bathroom. Once they came inside, Austin would put Radar's harness on, attach his leash, and get ready to take his dog for a walk. Austin's mom or dad would always help him, as walking around the block by yourself when you are only six years old is not always the safest thing to do. For Austin, it felt like a fun way to spend time with his parents before the day got started.

Once they got home, Austin made sure Radar had plenty of food, water, and toys to keep him going through the afternoon. He also made sure to shut the door to all of the bedrooms, as Radar was just a puppy, and sometimes he would go in there and chew things that he was not supposed to be chewing. When he was ready to go, Austin would give Radar a big hug and leave for school.

When Austin got home, there were still plenty of chores to do so that he could take care of Radar! He would refill his food and water, and once again put a harness and leash on Radar so they could take him for his afternoon walk. If Radar went to the bathroom on that walk, Austin would have to pick it up with a bag so he could put it in the garbage.

After they got home, Austin would take Radar in the backyard and throw a ball for him to help Radar get all of his energy out. Then, he would take out the training treats and teach Radar new tricks. Austin taught Radar how to sit, lie down, jump, bark on command, and shake a paw. Every day, they would practice a new trick, so Radar could learn something cool and interesting.

Before bed, Austin would have to play with Radar again to make sure Radar was good and tired, so he would sleep through the night. He would throw the ball for him, teach him more tricks, and sometimes take him for another walk if his dad was home from work. Then, he would tuck Radar in so he could go to sleep in his very own bed.

Whenever Radar got sick, Austin would have to take Radar to the vet. He also had to take Radar to the vet for his puppy checkups and annual checkups, as well as to get him his shots. Taking proper care of his dog was an important way to make sure his friend was always happy, healthy, and well cared for.

Austin loved having a dog, but having his very own dog taught him that puppies were a lot of work! Still, Austin knew that his best friend was worth it, and was happy that his parents let him have his new best friend. For the rest of their lives together, Austin always cherished and cared for Radar the very best he could, which is why Radar lived a long, happy, and healthy life.

Chapter 10: Chelsea Discovers Consistency

Chelsea really wanted to be the best scorer on the basket team, but no matter how hard she tried, it always seemed like she couldn't do it. Every Thursday, Chelsea would practice with her teammates, yet no matter how hard she tried, she could barely score one basket. Eventually, Chelsea got upset and wanted to quit playing basketball.

"You can't quit playing!" Her friends argued. "I have to; I'm no good." She sighed.

When her coach heard she wanted to quit, she tried to help Chelsea feel better about her ability to play. "Chelsea, I heard you want to quit. Before you do, I want you to try one thing for me. When you go home after school every day, try scoring baskets at home. See how well you do!" Her coach said. "But how will that make me any better?" Chelsea asked. "You will see. If I'm wrong, I will let you quit." Her coach smiled.

Every day after school, Chelsea went home and practiced playing basketball.

For the first week, Chelsea was terrible at it. She saw no improvement. In fact, she may have gotten worse because she was not used to the hoop she had at home.

After that week, though, Chelsea got better.

At first, she only got a little better.

Over time, she was scoring every single basket.

Chelsea showed up at school the following week, ready to show off her new skills. Her teammates were shocked to see her improvement, but her coach was not.

"I knew you could do it!" Her coach smiled.

"Thank you, coach!" Chelsea said, scoring another basket.

"You see, consistency really does pay off." Coach said.

"What does it mean to be consistent?" Chelsea asked.

"It means you keep doing it over and over again until you get the results you want." Her coach taught her.

"I love consistency!" Chelsea cheered, scoring yet another basket. Now, she had what it took to be the best scorer on the team.

Chapter 11: Barney Becomes Brave

Barney was afraid of bees. He was so afraid of bees that anytime he saw them; he would scream and run in the opposite direction.

"I don't like bees!" he would yell, running away.

One day, Barney's dad wanted to show him that bees were not scary. He also wanted to show Barney how to be brave around his fears.

Barney's dad took him outside, and together they found a bee. Right before Barney screamed and ran away, Barney's dad said, "Look! I want to show you something cool!" So, Barney looked.

At first, Barney was scared. Then, he saw his dad take the bee and bring it into the house. Barney was surprised. Barney's dad put the bee in a little cup and told him to look at it, so he did. As he looked in, Barney saw the little fuzzy bee crawling around inside the cup. At first, he thought the bee looked scary. As he kept watching, though, the bee kept moving around, and Barney started to think that the bee looked cute.

After a few minutes, Barney's dad let the bee out of the cup and asked Barney to carry it back out to the garden. Barney was scared and did not want to, but his dad assured him he would be okay because male bumblebees do not bite, and this was a male bumblebee. Finally, Barney agreed and let the little bee crawl on his finger. Then, he carefully walked outside and put the bee on a flower in the garden.

"Was that so bad?" his dad asked.

"No!" Barney smiled, looking at the bee.

"Well done for being brave, Son!" His dad cheered, high fiving Barney.

Chapter 12: Talia Learns About Team Work

Talia was a good, strong worker. She always finished her homework on time, could score a goal at any sport, and was the best on her team no matter what game she played. There was only one problem: Talia was bad at sharing.

When they played team sports, Talia never shared the ball with anyone else. She would hog the ball and avoid passing it to anyone else, hoarding all of the shots for herself. When coach called on everyone to pick their positions, Talia would pick offense every time so she could be the one leading the team to scores. Talia loved being in control and guiding her team to success.

In class, group projects never went well, either. Talia would not let anyone else do any work, and would instead do everything herself. Talia would do the research, write everything down, create the projects, and hand them in. When it came time to grade everything, Talia would tell the teachers that she did all the work because her teammates refused to help. This was a lie, but the teachers did not know better.

One day, Talia told her teacher this very lie, and her group member spoke up.

"That is not true!" She said.

"Yes it is!" Talia said.

"No! We tried to help, but you did not let us." Her classmate insisted.

"Is this true?" The teacher asked.

"No!" Talia argued.

"Yes." All her group members said.

"Talia, that is not nice. You have to share the responsibility, that is the point of group projects. You need to learn to work together with others." Her teacher said.

The next day, Talia's teacher made her do another group project. This time, her teacher showed her how to work with a team. Talia's teacher showed her how to let other's research, write, and build the project with her. At first, Talia did not like sharing. Soon, she realized it was much easier when she had her friends helping her, so she welcomed the help of her team members.

Once Talia learned to work as a team member, she wanted to work as a team on *everything*. With homework, she happily let her group members help her. When she was on the sports field, she shared the ball and offered her team a chance to play. Even at home Talia was a better team player, as she let her siblings take part in the things they were doing together.

Talia realized that being a team player was so fun because they got way more done, and they all won. By the end, Talia *loved* teamwork!

PART III

1
POEMS ABOUT GOOD FEELINGS

Happy

I went to see my friend,
His name was Carter Blue.
He liked to play with blocks,
And I kind of like them, too.

We play all day together,
Smiles ear to ear,
And when we play, I have to say,
I could stay all year.

Carter is my buddy,
We even share our snack.
Sometimes I take his toy,
But I always give it back.

We sit and watch a movie,
Or maybe play a game,
But sometimes we just sit,
And I feel good, just the same.

On days when I get bored,
It's Carter that I call,
He'll always make me feel good,
We always have a ball.

And that's what I call happy,
Warm and safe and free,
That's how I feel with Carter,
And happy works for me.

Excited

Today is the day that I get to go
Up on the ride where just big kids go.

It goes super high up to the sky
And now I could cry, "It's my turn, oh my!"

I wait in the line that goes all around.
I stand on my toes, don't want to touch ground.

"I see it, I see it! It's here, yes it is!"
I am jumping and clapping, like soda I fizz.

I know it is close now, coming so quick.
"It's me, it's me! It's me you should pick!"

They wave me to go now, my waiting is done,
I climb on the ride, ready for fun!

"You must be excited," my mom says to me.
Excited is right, but I just say, "Weeeee!"

Calm

I sit on the sofa with my good friend Bear,
I know he's not real, but I do not care.

He is so fuzzy, brown and kind.
He cannot talk, but I do not mind.

Next I find blanket, pull it up close,
This is the part that I like the most.

I do not move, I do not wiggle,
I do not play, I do not giggle.

This is the time when I can sit still,
You think that I can't, but I know I will.

My dad says I'm calm, and that could be right,
But I do not care, as I sit here all night.

Silly

Come with me, you should see,
Watch me go so crazy!
Going up, going down,
Turning flips like a clown!

Watch this skip,
Watch this hop,
Watch me go,
I can't stop!

Then a joke, then a poke,
Then a clap and a tap,
Then I roll on the floor,
Laugh until I am sore.

Do you want to see more?
Oh, I have much more!

Did you see, see my face?
Now let's go have a race!
I zoom here, I zoom there,
Come and catch me, if you dare!

Do a dance, next I prance,
Do a shake, eat some cake.
Am I done? No way, pal!
I am one silly gal.

Surprised

School is now over,
It's finally done,
And all I want now,
Is some fun in the sun.

I walk to the bus,
I hop up the step,
"Hey, good day, Fred?"
And I say back, "Yep!"

I get to my door,
And open it slow,
See, it's my birthday,
You know how birthdays go!

Soon I'll have gifts,
And plenty of food,
Maybe a cake?
I'm in the mood!

But no one is home,
The lights are not on,
Where is my family?
Could they be gone?

I walk room to room,
Not sure what to do,
When all of a sudden,
I hear, "Yoohoo!"

The lights now flash on,
And I see everyone,
They're yelling "Surprise!"
And I say, "Time for fun!"

2
POEMS ABOUT THE PLAYGROUND

Monkey Bars

Grab this one,
Grab that one,
Keep going,
Must have fun.

Grab again,
Grab both hands,
Don't give up,
I must land.

Grab the bar,
Grab so far,
I might fall,
Fall so far.

Grab with care,
Grab the air,
Down I go,
It's not fair!

Scrape my knee,
Scratch my face,
Cry some tears,
Hate this place!

Then my mom,
Nice and calm,
Comes to say,
"Hey, come on!"

"We all fall,
Yes, yes all,
It's okay,
You are small."

"It takes time,
You will find,
You can try,
Make up your mind."

"You can play,
That's okay,
You will do it,
Do it someday."

I sit and sigh,
"I guess I'll try…"
I go across!
"I can!" I cry.

Swings

I am sitting,
Sitting on the swing,
And as I get ready,
I start to sing.

"Here we go up,
Up to the sky,
And if we push hard,
We can go high!"

"I push my legs up,
I push my legs down,
I want to see clouds,
Not see the ground."

I start to swing faster,
Kicking so quick,
Soon I'll be there,
Lickety-split!

I want to touch blue,
Want to go soar,
Want to get there,
Want to see more.

If I go high,
Then I can be,
Just like a bird,
Happy and free.

I sing it again,
And I sing it so loud,
This time I know,
I will reach a cloud.

Slides

I climb up the rungs,
Filling my lungs,
This will be great!
I cannot wait!

I'm at the top,
No need to stop,
Take a look down,
Then kind of frown.

It's kind of high…
I don't want to cry…
My friends will all see…
I could hurt my knee…

I look to the left,
No one.
I look to the right,
No one.

I take a big step,
My mind is now set,
I can do this,
I will not miss.

Now I will sit,
And slowly I tip,
Should I let go?
Slide high to low?

I do it, too late!
And hey, this is great!
I *can* take the slide!
It is one great ride!

Seesaw

When you go up,
I go down,
When you go high,
I touch the ground.

It's back and forth,
It's you and me,
The two of us,
Are so happy.

I push up hard,
You go down fast,
I laugh a lot,
I hope it lasts!
We can't stop now,

It's fun and free,
We love this game,
We're so happy.

We want to play,
A new fun game,
It looks like here,
But not the same.

We're on a ship!
The sea is high,
We can't fall off,
You and I.

We rock about,
Both high and low,
But overboard,
We cannot go.

So hold on tight,
The ship will rise,
The waves will crash,
The sun will rise.

And now the waves,
Begin to slow,
We're safe home now,
No need to row.

We did so well,
We did it, friend.
Now let's hop off,
That's the end!

Jump Rope

Watch me jump this rope,
Think I'll fall? Nope!

I can rock this thing.
Move my legs like wings.

They flap down and up,
I never mess it up.

The rope goes round and round,
Slapping on the ground.

I count and count some more,
I try to keep my score.

I cannot keep going,
I show no sign of slowing.

Jumping is my jam
Grab that rope and BAM!

This girl cannot be stopped,
My score cannot be topped!

This rope and I will win,
I wear a nice big grin.

Jumping is my game,
Sandra is my name.

Hey, just watch my feet.
I cannot be beat.

Want to try it now?
Beat me? I don't know how!

3
POEMS ABOUT FRIENDSHIP

Friend

So I like you,
And you like me,
We like to play,
As you can see.

We like robots,
And big toy cars,
We like our blocks,
And dinosaurs.

And if you cry,
I will come,
To see what's wrong,
Make sure it's done.

And if I fall,
I know you'll be,
Right there real soon,
You will help me.

You make me laugh.
You make me smile.
You make me happy,
For a long while.

So that's a friend,
Someone who's there,
They always come,
They show they care.

Sometimes you fight,
Sometimes you cry,
But it will stop,
When they come by.

Good friends you keep,
Good friends stay near,
Good friends are special,
Good friends are dear.

Making New Friends

I really want a friend,
A playing pal for me,
I really want a friend,
Is it so hard to see?

But how do I get started?
How do I find someone?
Do I shout, "Be my friend!"
Or poke them and then run?

No, that isn't right,
I can't find nobody.
I am stuck alone,
Bored without a buddy.

Then my dad comes by,
He says, "What's got you sad?"
I don't know what to say…
"I've got no friends, it's bad!"

He says, "Now just you wait,
That cannot be true,
Everyone would want,
An awesome friend like you."

He says, "Let's fix this now,
I think I've got a plan,
You will make a friend,
You'll do it, yes you can!"

"First, you walk up close,
But not too close, you see,
And then you say, 'Hello!'
And they may smile, maybe."

"And if they smile at you,
You can say some more,
Like, 'Do you want to play?'
That's what this ball is for."

"Take this ball with you,
And squeeze it nice and tight,
You can squeeze so hard,
Squeeze with all your might."

"Making friends is scary,
Making friends is tough,
But when you squeeze that ball,
Remember, you're great stuff."

"If they will be your friend,
I'll be pumped for you,
And if they say no thanks,
You'll know what to do."

"You can come find me,
We will take a walk,
I'm a friend, you see,
And we can always talk."

Talk Time

"Hey!"
"Hello!"
"Ready?"
"Let's go!"

It's play time with Charlotte,
Play time again,
Time to see Charlotte!
I do a quick spin.

Charlotte is funny,
Charlotte is cool,
Charlotte likes baseball,
Crayons, and pools.

Then I see Charlotte,
And it's kind of weird…
I can't find my words!
It's just like I feared!

I want my friend,
To see I'm so chill,
I am the coolest,
But I just stand still…

How do I talk?
How do I walk?
How do I speak?
Can I just squeak?

Then Charlotte says,
"Um…should we play?"
And I can say, "Yes!"
She saved the day!

Good or Bad?

I have a friend,
They are so great,
Well, I think they are…
But then again…wait…

Does a good friend
Ask you to cheat?
Do they throw food
They don't want to eat?

Do they make sounds
During calm time?
Tell you it's apple
When really it's lime?

I just don't know,
This is not right,
A good friend is kind,
A friend does what's right.

I have a friend,
They are so great,
Well, I think they are…
But then again…wait…

Does a good friend
Always take turns?
Bring you a band aid
If you have burns?

Does a good friend
Share things with you?
Tell you great stories,
Tell you what's true?

That's a good friend,
Now I can see,
Because a good friend
Will look out for me.

Saying Goodbye

It's moving day,
But somehow I'm sad.
I should feel happy,
But I just feel bad.

Our new house is big,
Our new house is fun,
I like my room,
But I don't want to come.

Lily won't be there.
Lily must stay.
Lily's my friend,
But we cannot play.

She will stay here,
I will move on,
I cannot do it,
She will be gone.

It is not fair,
It is not nice,
I'd rather get sick,
I'd rather have lice.

She is my best friend,
Really, the best,
Not like my other friends,
Not like the rest.

We pull away,
The truck is now going,
I start to wave,
But I am crowing.

"What about Lily?
What will I do?"
Then my mom says,
"You can start new."

Old friends are great,
Old friends are true,
But new friends can come,
New, just for you."

4

POEMS ABOUT FUNKY FEELINGS

Anxiety

Today is the big game,
Today they chant my name.

It is all up to us,
We cannot cry or fuss.

I must help us win,
I must lift my chin.

"Do it!" they all say,
"Do it! Go and play!"

But what if I cannot?
What if I freeze and stop?

What if I cannot score?
What if they ask for more?

Will I be called so cool,
Or will I be a fool?

I take a breath so deep,
I close my eyes, don't peep.

This is too much for me,
Why can't they let me be?

I'm jumpy, worried, mad,
And maybe a little sad.

This is anxiety,
It lives inside of me.

It makes me doubt myself,
Want to hide up on a shelf.

But I will work, not quit,
Someday I'll conquer it.

Embarrassment

It's show time,
Show off time,
It's my line…
Oh no…mine!

It's too late,
I just hate,
That I choke,
My voice broke.

They all see,
I'm stuck, me,
And I freeze,
Don't even sneeze.

They all stare,
They all care,
Their smiles show,
The whispers grow.

I messed it up!
I've given up!
I cannot do it,
Cannot get through it!

Don't look at me,
Just let me be.
Just make it stop
So I can plop.

I want to sit,
Sit and forget,
My face turns red,
I want my bed.

Then I could hide,
Go deep inside,
All warm and safe,
Far from the hate.

Mistakes can happen,
They keep on coming,
But you get up,
Dust off, get tough.

Mistakes are fine,
Forget the line.
And soon you'll find,
They don't really mind.

Shyness

It's school today,
I have to go.

It's school today,
But I won't show.

It's school today,
But I will hide.

It's school today,
But I'm inside.

At home,
It's quiet,
No one to joke.

At home,
It's nice,
No one to poke.

At home,
It's safe,
No one to hurt me.

At home,
It's fun,
No one to leave me.

But school has kids,
And I like kids.

But school has friends,
And I want friends.

But school has toys,
And I like toys.

But school has recess,
And I want recess.

I'm sorry,
I don't talk,
But I can walk.

I'm sorry,
I don't run,
But I still like fun.

I'm sorry,
I'm still shy,
But friends come, let's say hi!

Stress

The test is coming soon,
The teacher says at noon.

I tried and tried to study,
I even called my buddy.

I stayed up late last night,
Got all the answers right.

And then I did my chores,
But think about high scores.

It's time to go do this,
There's nothing I can miss.

I must go here, go there,
I cannot stop to stare.

I must do everything,
No time to top and sing.

I must get it done,
Before the bell has rung.

It's time to take the test,
I think and try my best.

Now off to get haircut.
Try again to cheer up.

There's just too much to do,
But I have to make it through.

Jealousy

You got the biggest toy,
I guess that it's okay.
But it belonged to me,
Just the other day.

You should not have it now,
It's really not for you,
You should hand it over,
You should, shouldn't you?

You see, I really want it,
I know that we should share,
But I like it and I saw it,
But take it, I don't care…

But the toy, it was for me,
It was my special treat,
And it's you who has it now,
I guess you got me beat.

Why should you get to hold it?
It's really not that great.
You don't really want it,
You should really wait.

Why did you take my toy?
It should be mine to keep.
We had a lot of fun,
It honks and turns and beeps.

Alright, I guess it's your now,
I guess I'll just move on.
But I'll still want my toy,
Even when it's gone

5
POEMS ABOUT PARENTS

Parents

They're sometimes nice,
Sometimes sweet,
Sometimes scary,
Sometimes neat.

I call them parents,
They seems to like it.
They call me "kiddo"
And I don't mind it.

They're sort of silly,
I like their smiles,
They do my laundry,
Make big piles.

I like their food,
Except the veggies,
They make my lunch,
In little baggies.

But there is more,
That makes them great,
So much to share,
I cannot wait.

They give big hugs,
They always mean it,
When I call home,
They know they're needed.

They gives their love,
Like they give food,
There's lots of it,
In every mood.

I'm sad,
They're there.
I'm bad,
They're there.

The best part of parents,
They're always there.

Not Inside the House!

I want to learn to ski.
Not inside the house!

I want to play football.
Not inside the house!

I want to waterslide.
Not inside the house!

I want to swing my bat.
Not inside the house!

I want to make mud pies.
Not inside the house!

I want to run around.
Not inside the house!

So many rules for me,
All inside the house.

There is no fun for me,
Not inside the house.

But skiing is on snow…
Not inside the house.

But football is on fields…
Not inside the house.

But waterslides are outside…
Not inside the house.

But bats are for baseball,
Not inside the house.

But mud pies are from dirt…
Not inside the house.

But running should go far…
Not stuck inside the house.
Because I Said So

My parents looked at me
And said just four short words.

"Because I said so!"
Those words could not be worse.

What do they even mean?
Does anybody know?

"Because I said so!"
Are you sure, though?

I have to ask you, "Why?"
I guess you have to say it.

"Because I said so!"
Is one way you can say it.

I guess I just don't see,
I guess I don't know how.

If I ask you why again,
Will you have a cow?

What do those four words mean?
Why do you say it so?

You take a big breath now,
I turn and start to go.

And then you say, "I love you.
And you should have the best."

"Sometimes I don't know why,
And so I say because."

"But all the things I say,
They come from all my love."

Time Out

They said it,
They said time out,
They said it,
And now I pout.

I hate time out,
It stinks.
I stand there,
Stand and think.

To stand here,
Is a bore.
To stand here,
Is a chore.

They time it,
Every time.
They make me stand,
On a line.

Why do I stand?
I ask.
They say,
Stay on task.

What's a task?
I'd like to know.
But it's time out,
They go.

I guess I'll stand,
Okay.
I'll stand,
I cannot play.

And then I start to think.
Why did they send me here?
And then I hear a whisper,
Right inside my ear.

I did something bad,
And I need to fix it.
Time out is my time,
To think and not to miss it.

Do This, Do That

You said I should study,
You said I should eat,
You said I should sleep,
You said wash your feet.

But why should I study?
And eat?
And sleep?
Why do I care
If my feet kind of stink?

You said I should wake up,
You said I should plan,
You said I should clean up,
You said give a hand.

But why should I wake up?
And plan?
And clean up?
Why do I care
If the room's messed up?

And then you talk back,
And now I can see.
You telling me to,
Is caring for me.

If I don't study,
And eat,
And sleep,
If I don't wake up,
And plan,
And clean up,

Life will be hard,
Life will be crazy,
When you say "Do this!"
You're thinking of me.

6
POEMS ABOUT SIBLINGS

Brothers and Sisters

I want to be alone,
But you are always there.

You like to tickle me,
Put old gum in my hair.

You never let me see,
You always get there first.

You get the coolest stuff,
You really are the worst.

Your door is always shut,
Sometimes it makes me scream.

You always shut me out,
It's really kind of mean.

But when the door is open,
When we sit and talk,
It's really kind of nice,
We play and laugh and walk.

When parents make us crazy,
And school is just so hard,
You grab my hand and say,
"Let's go play in the yard."

When the day is done,
And you are still by me,
I look at you and think,
"This is the way to be."

It's MY Room!

I said,
DON'T come in.

I said,
DON'T touch.

I said,
DON'T visit.

Did I ask too much?

You can be…
Boring.

You can be…
A bug.

You can be…
Loud.

I said DON'T pull the plug!

You don't seem to get it.

You really must not see.

I don't want you in here.

DON'T spend time with me.

How come you do not know?

And why DON'T you just go?

I guess,
You can be cute.

I guess,
You can be sweet.

I guess,
You can be funny.

I guess,
You're kind of neat.

Okay, you can come in.

Okay, you can touch.

Okay, you can visit.

You DON'T ask too much.

Oh, Brother

You're such a bother, brother.
You scream and kick and cry.

You're such a bother brother,
I hang my head and sigh.

You're such a bother, brother,
You never can sit still.

You're such a bother, brother,
You sound so loud and shrill.

You're such a bother, brother,
You poke me way too much.

You're such a bother, brother,
You make me want to punch.

But then you say my name.
Oh, brother.

Then we play a game.
Oh, brother.

You giggle when I tickle,
Oh, brother.

You even share your pickle,
Oh, brother.

You give hug me big each day,
Oh brother.

I'm so glad you'll stay,
Oh, brother.

Tips for Sisters

When you have a sister,
    It can be a lot.

She may take all the candy,
    She may bang on a pot.

When you have a sister,
    You can get real mad.

She may break your toy,
    Or the doll you had.

When you have a sister,
    She may get the time.

Parents can forget you,
    Just like a lost dime.

When you have a sister,
    It can be so cool.

She may say, "Hello!"
    In the hall at school.

When you have a sister,
    You can get real sad.

But she will come to save you,
    Take away the bad.

When you have a sister,
Your parents may just see.
It's nice to have a sister,
Someone who will love me.

Siblings At School

You see your sister,
See your brother,
They're walking down the hall.

You say, "Hi!"
They walk by,
Like you're not real at all.

They are older,
You are younger,
They don't want to see.

You don't get it,
You are sad,
"Why don't they talk to me?"

They are cool,
You are not,
Guess it's just the rule.

You say nothing,
They keep walking,
No fun times at school.

Kids are mean,
Call you names,
You don't know what to do.

You start crying,

It's not fair,
But then they come to you.

You see your sister,
See your brother,
And they say, "What's wrong?"

They take your hand,
You both stand,
And then you walk along.

7
POEMS ABOUT BAD FEELINGS

Anger

You took it,
I know it,
And it's not okay.

You broke it,
I know it,
I'll get you today.

You lost it,
I know it,
And now you will pay.

You did it,
I know it,
I'll not let you stay.

I'm hot,
I'm panting,
I'm red,
I'm clenching.

You hurt me,
I know it,
And you have to go.

You hit me,
I know it,
I'll make sure you know.

You pinched me,
I know it,
And now my eyes glow.

You tripped me,
I know it,
And you'll take a blow.

I'm angry,
I'm mad,
I'm upset,
It's bad.

Anger hits,
Anger hurts,
Anger yells,
Anger blurts.

Don't let it take you,
Don't let it grow,
Don't let it hurt you,
Let anger go.

Frustration

I'm sitting in math,
It looks all squiggly.
I'm in my chair,
But I'm getting wiggly.

This is too hard,
This is just crazy,
Don't call me stupid!
Don't call me lazy!

I want to get it,
Really I do,
But it is so long,
Does it make sense to you?

I'm sitting in reading,
It looks all wrong,
I'm on the carpet,
But I can't sit long.

This is too hard,
This is just crazy,
Don't call me stupid!
Don't call me lazy!

I want to read,
Really I do,
But words look like noodles,
Does it make sense to you?

I guess I'm frustrated,
I don't understand,
Could you please help me?
Please take my hand.

Sadness

One day, she left,
My cat named Kitty.

She was so fluffy,
She was so pretty.

One day, she left,
And now I am here.

She was the best,
She always sat near.

One day, she left.
Now what to do?

She was my friend,
Played with me, too.

One day, she left,
Then came the tears.

She used to snuggle,
She stopped my fears.

Today, I sit,
All by myself.

I see her toy,
Up on the shelf.

Today, I cry,
Sit on the rug.

I see her bed,
Give it a hug.

Today, I hide,
It's nice and dark.

I see her window,
The scratches she'd mark.
Today, I'm sad,
No way around it.

For now, I am lost,
But I'll come out of it.

FEAR!

I was walking
Down hall
When I saw
Something crawl.

It was big,
It was hairy,
It was mean,
It was SCARY!

I ran screaming,
Yelled so much,
Tripped on stairs,
Fell a bunch.

I was shaking
In my shoes
When I saw
Something move.

It was huge,
It was sneaky,
It was red,
It was CREEPY!

I ran screaming,
Eyes so wide,
Tried to find,
A place to hide.

I was hiding
In my room

When I saw
Something zoom.

It was tall,
It was grimy,
It was blue,
It was SLIMY!

Sometimes we can get so scared
We don't look to see what's there.
Sometimes toys have scary faces
If they sit in the wrong places.

So take a look
And don't get scared.
No need to fear
There's nothing there.

Grumpy

I don't want to,
Don't ask me,
I don't want to,
Let me be.

I'm not mad,
I'm not sad,
I'm not bored,
I'm not glad.

I'm just grumpy,
Feelings all lumpy.

I don't like it,
Yes, it's true,
I don't like it,
I *used* to.

I'm not sleepy,
I'm not crazy,
I'm not goofy,
I'm not lazy.

I'm just grumpy,
Feelings all lumpy.

When you don't know what to feel,
And you just want to snap,
You don't want to smile,

You don't want to clap,

Know that it's okay,
We all get this way.

When you can't get all happy,
And you just want to frown,
You don't want to play,
You don't want to clown,

Know that it's okay,
We all get this way.
Sometimes we just get grumpy,
Riding feelings can get bumpy.

8
POEMS ABOUT SCHOOL

First Day

It's my first day,
My first day at school.

I check out my shoes,
Make sure they look cool.

It's my first day,
And I am so excited.

I peek into the room,
I smile, I can't hide it.

It's my first day,
And I go find my seat.

It is by my friend,
And I think that's neat.

It's my first day,
And it is all so new.

I look up at the teacher,
To see what we will do.

It's my first day,
New shirt, new shorts, new hair.
I feel like I look good,
Like a superhero would.

It's my first day,
I know that I'm so smart.

And on this first day,
I am ready to start.

Teacher

Look, it's the teacher!
They look so tall.

Look, it's the teacher!
And now I feel small.

Will they like me?
Are they kind?
I talk soft,
Will they mind?

Will they be good?
Are they fast?
I need help,
Will I last?

Look, it's the teacher!
They smile at me.

Look, it's the teacher!
And now I feel free.

I will talk soft,
They will be kind,
I will need help,
And they won't mind.

I will be fast,
They will be cool,
I can go slow,
Hey, I love school!

Look, it's a teacher!
A helper on the way.

Look, it's a teacher!
I know they'll save the day.

My Desk

I have a desk,
It's at the back.

The top is brown,
The legs are black.

It has a lid,
It just lays there.

It has a scratch,
But I don't care.

Inside is stuff,
And it's all mine.

It's all a mess,
But it is fine.

There is a book,
And then a pen.

A paper, too,
I look again.

I find some gum,
And then a stick.

There is a toy,
I hide it quick!

The lid is stuck,
The teacher looks.

I push the toy,
I grab my books.

I shut the lid,
I look up fast.

The teacher talks,
I made it past!
My desk is old,
It's kind of rusty.

But it holds lots,
My desk is trusty.

Carpet Time

We go to the carpet,
We sit in a square.

We go to the carpet,
Teacher's in a chair.

We go to the carpet,
It is time to read.

We go to the carpet,
Learn the things we need.

We go to the carpet,
Sit and try to see.

We go to the carpet,
Hope they call on me!

Carpet time is funny,
We get to make noise.

Carpet time is busy,
We can play with toys.

Carpet time is chatty,
We can talk sometimes.

Carpet time is sitting,
Learn to count the dimes.

Carpet time is happy,
We can sit by friends.

Carpet time is so cool,
Hope it never ends!

Class Time

I come in,
I sit down.
Read my book,
Then I frown.

What is next?
What to do.
I look up,
Find a clue!

First is math,
Next we leave,
Off to art
Or P.E.!

Then we read,
Take a break,
Pick our lunch,
What to take?

Read aloud
Is the best,
Science time,
Last a test!

Math class time
Is so cool.
We make shapes
And count, too.

Art is fun,
Learn to color.
P.E.'s neat,
Tag each other.

Books we read
Wait on shelves.
I see princes,
I see elves.

Teacher reads,
Reads some more,
It is super,
Not a bore.

Science time's
Kind of nuts!
Make a mess,
Poke at stuff.

What a day!
Lots to do!
Let's get started!
See what's new!

9
POEMS ABOUT FOOD

Salad

I look at my plate,
What is that I see?

Kind of looks like grass…
But that cannot be.

Then I see a red thing,
Round and slimy, too.

You say it's tomato,
But I just say, "Ew!"

There is a white river
Falling down the grass.

You tell me it's ranch,
But I think I'll pass.

Then I find an orange stick,
Sitting in the goo.

That is called a carrot?
And I eat that, too?

No, you must be crazy,
This is not for me.
I do not eat salads,
I'm a kid, you see?

You want me to try that?
Put it to my lips?

Open up and take it?
Can't I lick the tip?

Fine, I guess I'll just try,
See what it's about…

Hey, it's kind of tasty!
I'm glad that I found out!

My Plate

It is time to eat,
Look down at my plate,
It is time to eat,
And I cannot wait.

It is time to eat,
I see lots to pick,
It is time to eat,
Better do it quick!

It is time to eat,
First my fruits and veggies,
It is time to eat,
I don't take too many.

It is time to eat,
Meat is what I see,
It is time to eat,
Just a bit for me.

It is time to eat,
Maybe I have bread,
It is time to eat,
Have to use my head.

It is time to eat,
Maybe I have sweets,
It is time to eat,

Those are special treats.

It is time to eat,
Look down at my plate.
It is time to eat,
And I cannot wait.

Candy

It's sweet,
It's sticky,
It's great,
Never icky.

I eat it,
Every day,
Grab some more,
But you say,

"Not so much,
That's too many,
You can't eat
So much candy!"

But it's sweet,
But it's sticky,
But it's great,
Never icky.

I eat more,
I can't stop,
Grab some more,
Lick my chops.

"You must stop,
Yes, you should,
No more now,
It's not good!"

Still it's sweet,
Still it's sticky,
Still it's great,
Never icky.

I just eat,
Eat all day,
But then I
Want to play.

"Hey, what's wrong?
I can't do things,
I can't run,
And I can't sing!"

It was sweet,
It was sticky,
It was great,
But I feel icky.

I'm too big,
I'm not happy,
I can't move,
I get snappy.

Candy's good,
Something to eat,
But just some,
Make it a treat.

Fruit

What is this yellow thing?
It's all thin and long.

This is a banana!
Peel it, bite it, gone.

What is this orange ball?
It's all soft and round.

This is called an orange!
It is sweet, I found.

What is this shiny thing?
It's all hard and red.

This is called an apple!
It's juicy, I said.

What is this big green ball?
It's stripes are up and down.

This is watermelon!
It grows on the ground.

What is this spiky stuff?
It's got lots of pokes.

This is pineapple!
It's so good, no joke.

What are these tiny things?
Blue and round and small.

These are called blueberries!
You could eat them all.

Snacks

Snack attack!

Did you see?
There are chips
Staring at me.

Snack attack!

Did you know?
See cookies,
Have to go.

Snack attack!

Did you guess?
Sweets for me
Are the best.

Snack attack!

Did you buy?
Got it all,
I can't lie.

Snack attack!

Did you look?
Got some pop,
Didn't cook.

Snack attack!

Did you peek?
Ate some cake
Each day this week.

Snack attack!

Snacks got me!
I'm too full,
Can't you see?

I need a meal,
But I feel,
Full of snacks.
Can't go back.

Snacks are cool,
Snacks at school,
Snacks you smash,
But then you crash.

Pick a fruit,
Pick a veggie,
Grab a snack,
But not just any.

10 POEMS ABOUT SHARING AND CARING

Sharing

First it's you,
Then it's me,
That is sharing
How it should be.

First I hold,
Then you hold,
That is sharing,
So I'm told.

First you go,
Then I go,
That is sharing,
That I know.

First I cross,
Then you cross,
That is sharing,
Don't be a boss.

First you zoom,
Then I zoom,
That is sharing
In my room.

First I read,
Then you read,
That is sharing,
Just what we need.

First you ride,
Then a ride,
That is sharing,
That I've tried.

First I play,
Then you play,
That is sharing,
Do it all day.

First you swing,
Then I swing,
That is sharing,
The best thing.

Taking Turns

You go first,
You go last,
It's okay,
We'll have a blast.

We take turns,
Because it's fair
We must take turns,
It's everywhere.

We wait in line,
We raise our hand,
Taking turns,
It's what we planned.

You get to go,
No matter what,
So wait your turn,
Please don't say, "But!"

There is no "but."
We must take turns.
We all will go.
We all must learn.

And if your turn,
It never comes,
Just try again,
You will get some.

We all need turns,
It keeps things cool,
So wait your turn,
When you're at school.

And wait your turn,
Just wait awhile,
Just wait your turn,
With a big smile.

Giving

This is for you,
I hope it will do.

I wanted to make it,
I tried not to break it.

It is not much,
But I worked a bunch.

I want you to have it,
It's kind of a rabbit.

I used lots of sticks,
Ones that I picked.

There's glitter and glue,
It's red, yellow, blue.

I made it with pink,
Your favorite, I think.

I have worked so hard,
And here, I made a card.

I wrote that inside,
I wrote it, I tried.

Please hold out your hand,
And watch my gift land.

This is all for you,
I hope it will do.

I give and feel good,
I give just like I should.

Helping

Let me help you,
I am here,
Let me help you,
Have no fear.

Let me help you,
It's okay.
Let me help you,
Every day.

Let me help you,
Help is great.
Let me help you,
Not too late.

*I don't need help,
I am smart.
I don't need help,
Don't you start.*

*I don't need help,
I can do it.
I don't need help,
I'll just do it.*

*I don't need help,
Help is bad,
I don't need help,
Makes me mad.*

We all need help,
Even you,
We all need help,
Yes, we do.

*I don't need help,
Help is lame!*

But when you're stuck,
Who's to blame?

Find some help,
Please don't frown.
Help is there,
When you fall down.

Caring

I see my friends around me,
They all stop and smile,
And with my friends around me,
I can rest awhile.

My friends will now take care of me,
My friends are good and kind, you see.

When I need care,
My friends are there,
That makes me so happy.

I see a friend who needs me,
I stop and help them out,
And when that friend is better,
We go play about.

My friend is now able to rest,
Caring for friends is what is best.

When they need care,
Then I am there,
So put me to the test.

I see my friends around me,
They will be right here,
And we care for each other,
So keep your good friends near.

www.ingramcontent.com/pod-product-compliance
Lightning Source LLC
Chambersburg PA
CBHW071620080526
44588CB00010B/1206